Summer of the Ladybugs

Early Seasons of Grief

MARILYN WRAGG

Cover Design by Alexis Wragg

ISBN: 979-8-218-22449-3

DEDICATION

To Mike

To Alexis

To Carolyn, Andy, Charlie, Miles, and Katie

To Fellow Climbers—especially Sharon, Rose, Lynn,
and my grandmothers (Dodla and Ma Maw)

To my Lubbock First Christian Church family,
special sisters in Christ, and extended personal family
on earth and in Heaven, whose blessings in my life
will extend through Eternity

To God, to Whom all glory belongs

CONTENTS

PROLOGUE

"Grandma, Daddy used to take me over to my school to hunt for ladybugs. Do you think we could do that?"

That simple request from my precious 8-year-old granddaughter melted my heart. The days of ladybug hunting that ensued over that summer brought healing, hope, and stirrings of the joy I knew eventually would return to our lives, even as I remained in the throes of grief over the death of her Daddy—my son David.

It has been seven years since that summer. Yet, to this day, I can close my eyes and vividly recall the many sensations—the fresh smell of summer, the beauty of the outdoors, the soothing warmth of summer days softened by the west Texas breeze, the soft feel of grass and clover, the tickle of ladybugs crawling over our hands, and the relaxed sense of time standing still as Alexis and I scoured promising areas all around town in search of ladybug treasure troves.

I ask myself why these memories have so strongly resurfaced this past month. I surmise it is because we are in the sixth week of the coronavirus stay-at-home lockdown. Life suddenly has become more relaxed, giving me more time to be alone and reflect. Much of that time has been spent outdoors, where the first hints of summer are teasing me with lengthening days, warmer temperatures, blooming flowers, and the feel and scents of impending summer. And, oh yes, I just saw my first ladybug of the season.

LATE FALL

Pain, Disbelief, and God's Mercy

"Dear God, David can't really be gone."

I have thought, mouthed, whispered, and cried out those words countless times over the past 7½ years.

The first time was when I awoke the November morning after David had passed away during the night. The last time was just a few days ago. The difference is that in those early days, the realization hit me multiple times each hour—each time with an accompanying pain in my gut that almost doubled me over, and each time with a sharp renewal of that initial, gut-wrenching sense of loss.

Some label that initial stage of grief denial, but denial sounds more to me like a conscious rejection of reality. Disbelief more accurately describes what I experienced. I did not deny what had happened, but my mind was incapable of grasping the new reality that my son was gone. I simply could not believe that David, the son I had deeply loved, cared for, and prayed for over the past 32 years, could be gone. I could not fathom that I would never again see him in this earthly life. And I could not imagine living the remainder of my earthly life without David there.

The rest of that fall was exceedingly hard because the pain and disbelief recurred again and again. Focusing on small tasks or company of friends and family would distract my mind for a bit, but as soon as my mind reengaged, the reality of David's passing would hit afresh. Again and again, I would think, mouth, whisper, or cry out, "Dear God, David can't really be gone."

> "Dear God, David can't really be gone."

Now, I want to clarify that my "Dear God…" was not just an expression, akin to the casual "OMG!" I was genuinely calling out to God.

Having been blessed to grow up in a home where God was revered, I cannot remember a time when I did not believe in and talk to God. My childhood faith had matured through time and testing, and most recently had dramatically mushroomed through David's three-year battle with cancer.

In the darkest of times, through the roller coaster of David's harsh treatment cycles, fleeting periods of hope, cancer recurrences, and his final battle, I clung for dear life to God.

I prayed for David's healing. I thanked God for every blessing in the lives of David and my family. I took every fear and heartbreak to God. I prayed for God's mercy and comfort over David and all his family.

And although my prayers for David's earthly healing were not answered, God's mercy and comfort were evidenced throughout. I could see many evidences at the time, and many more have become clear over time as the fog of grief has lifted.

I sensed in the depth of my being that God's mercy had all along covered Mike and me and our family. I trusted that God's mercy had covered David through his final days to the moment he passed to Heaven. I believed that God's mercy would carry us through.

I claimed the promise of Romans 15:13: *"May the God of hope fill you with all joy and peace as you trust in Him, so you may overflow with hope through the power of the Holy Spirit."*

The week that David passed, I took long walks along the streets near Baylor Medical Center in Dallas while praying over and over, "God, if David should die, I know we will miss him terribly. I know we will grieve bitterly. But please, even as we grieve, let us not lose hope. Give us glimmers of hope even in our fog of grief. Please, God. Don't let us lose our hope."

God gave us hope that life would eventually be renewed on the other side of grief.

God was faithful to answer that prayer. Even in the deepest throes of grief, Mike and I were able to see God's hand. God blessed us with multitudes of friends and family who loved and supported us. He gave us ongoing purpose.

God gave us hope that life would eventually be renewed on the other side of grief. We knew David would want us to carry on and enjoy life, and we prayed daily for God to help us do so in tribute to him. Our grandchildren were the most precious reminders that life would go on, and times with Charlie, Miles, and Alexis were among the few times that the pain of loss retreated to the back of my mind for any length of time.

And yet… there was no shortcut through those first months. My heart clung to God, my spirit reached out for hope, but my mind could not yet make sense of the reality that David could be gone. Each morning I woke up as if my world had not forever changed, only to be hit once again with the realization that it had.

> Each morning I woke up as if my world had not forever changed, only to be hit once again with the realization that it had.

"Dear God, David can't really be gone."

WINTER

One Foot in Front of the Other, Routine, and Mornings in God's Word

Soon after David's passing, a friend's husband died after a brief illness. When I visited the next morning, she asked me as she was so desperately hurting, "How could you possibly have gotten through this?" My answer before I hugged her was, "One step at a time. One foot in front of the other."

That advice pretty much summed up how I made it through the first winter— relying on God as I took one step at a time, one foot in front of the other.

> "One step at a time. One foot in front of the other."

I literally focused on one small task at a time. Get out of bed. Take your shower. Go downstairs and do your morning exercises. Then came the one part to which I looked forward with any degree of joy—my daily routine of coffee, devotional, and Bible study time.

One thing I had learned while staying with David in the hospital is that routine can be a welcome friend in stressful times. In the course of cancer treatments, David had undergone two stem-cell transplants, which necessitated weeks of hospitalization and recovery in a city away from home. The bone-marrow transplant unit at Baylor Medical Center in Dallas allowed—in fact, required—a family member to live-in with the patient. So, David's wife and I traded off staying with him.

Days went remarkably fast during those many days of rooming with David. I think God was already training me for one foot in front of the other. As I continued from a distance to fulfill many church responsibilities, focusing on one task at a time was a blessed distraction from worry.

Church tasks, communicating with the many people checking on David, working through a couple Bible studies, taking long walks, praying for all the folks on the church prayer list, writing prayer articles for our church newsletter, and miscellaneous other "to-dos" occupied my mind and expended enough energy that sleep each night was a welcome rest.

Of course, my main focus was caring for and encouraging David. But my son was determined to retain his independence and not burden anyone. Honestly, I would have loved as a mom to have coddled and pampered him more, but I held the utmost respect for his stoic determination. I also understood that his determined independence kept David resolutely motivated when he could understandably have given in to the suffering he had to endure.

My morning routine of devotional and Bible study had thankfully been firmly established for a number of years. But it was during those hospital mornings that coffee assumed its integral place. Baylor Medical Center had several good coffee places, and I began to look forward each morning to trekking over to one of them for my morning brew, flavored with just the perfect amount of cream and sugar. I would bring it back to the room, where David would be waiting. On those mornings I was reluctant for any reason to leave him, he would muster a grin and say, "Momma, go on your little walk and get your coffee. I know you enjoy it, and I'll be fine."

Fast forward to that first winter after David's passing, and every morning when I brewed and flavored my cup of coffee, I would remember David encouraging me to enjoy the daily coffee routine. Thus began a practice that continues to this day: as I prepare to drink that first sip, I raise my coffee cup, look up, and smilingly say, "Cheers, David. Your Momma does still enjoy her morning coffee, and I think of you every time I do."

> Routine can be a welcome friend in stressful times.

That winter after David passed, I found that my newly entrenched routine of exercise, coffee, devotional, and Bible study consumed a lot more time than my previous morning schedule, so I began to set my wakeup alarm to allow at least two hours before any scheduled commitment. Those two hours went a long way towards setting the tone for the day, as I found myself encouraged by my ability to get through the first hours of each day with positive focus and minimum effort.

The next daily steps remained a challenge, and I reverted to my one-step-at-a-time mantra. Now, get dressed and ready for the day. Write a few thank-you notes. Check emails. Make your grocery list. Go to the store. Fix lunch… And so on through the day.

As I put one foot in front of the other through each day, one day led to another, and then another. And in spite of regularly being ambushed by grief, having a basic routine and meaningful tasks to accomplish helped me through that darkest of winters. I was usually just tired enough to be ready for bed.

God blessed me with the ability most nights to look forward to bedtime and then to sleep well. There were those occasional nights when I would wake up with an overwhelming sense of dread and loss. And I learned when that happened, the best thing to do was get up, go curl up in my cozy prayer nook, recite a psalm or words to a hymn, or cry as I spoke to God. Most times, I was eventually able to go back to bed and to sleep.

And although I still awoke many mornings having forgotten that David was gone, the anticipation of heading downstairs to morning coffee and my devotional time became a source of comfort.

SPRING

One Week at a Time, Serving Others, and Rejecting Self-Pity

It was a major breakthrough when I began to plan for a week at a time instead of one day at a time. Every Sunday evening, I set aside time to pray over my calendar for the upcoming week. Then, I made a cheat sheet that covered every day, so I would not overlook anything. I had learned the hard way that grief clouds one's mind, and it is all too easy to forget even important commitments. It is also easy to lose track of time—sometimes even forgetting what day of the week it is.

On my cheat sheet, I listed things to accomplish under two categories: "Family" and "Serving God." At the bottom, I made a simple chart for Monday through Sunday, with scheduled commitments written down for each day.

I kept, and still keep, this weekly schedule on my kitchen cabinet. I refer to it each evening,

> Grief clouds one's mind, and it is all too easy to forget even important commitments.

looking especially for any commitments I need to plan around the next day. Each following morning, I recheck before starting my daily routine. An unexpected bonus was that marking off completed objectives gave me a small sense of accomplishment, and I often thanked God for helping me get through much of my list.

I also thanked God that I had meaningful tasks to do and that He enabled me to get them done. Looking back, it seems remarkable to me that I was able to continue the church tasks that had always given me such fulfillment.

I had a noticeably difficult time making decisions; my mind was simply dull. For example, as much as I looked forward to visiting my daughter and her family in California, making arrangements and packing for each trip were mentally exhausting.

> I had a noticeably difficult time making decisions; my mind was simply dull.

God gave me the sense to say "no" to any new commitment during that season. But He graced me with strength to fulfill the commitments already in place. And as I fulfilled them, focusing on others in the process, I was able to experience brief periods when grief was noticeably lighter. I also felt hopeful in that I was making small steps forward.

One of my commitments for years had been visiting church members and friends in the hospital. It was one of the tasks that gave me great joy, as people were typically so very appreciative of visits, and several meaningful relationships were developed through visits with people I had prior known only casually.

I was ready to get back to my weekly visitation routine. However, I was unprepared for the wave of depression that hit me when I first stepped back into a hospital corridor. A panorama of memories flooded through my mind of that roller coaster of medical tests and treatment and hospital stays which led eventually to David's passing. Tears sprung into my eyes, and I shot up a desperate prayer, "God, I want to do this. I think You want me to do this. But it reminds me so very sadly of David. Please help me!"

Immediately, an answering thought sprang vividly into my mind, "There are no hospitals in Heaven." Along with that thought came an image of David whole and healed and joyful. I also recalled those people who had visited him during those extended hospital stays in Dallas, and how he had perked up and joked and entertained each and every visitor.

"There are no hospitals in Heaven."

I knew then that it would be ok, and it was. Not only were visits healing for me, but I found that my experiences with David gave me deepened connections with people whose illnesses were especially critical. I experienced firsthand the truth of the Scripture, *"Praise be to the God and Father of our Lord Jesus Christ, the Father of compassion and the God of all comfort, who comforts us in all our troubles, so that we can comfort those in any trouble with the comfort we ourselves receive from God"* (2 Corinthians 1:3–4).

God kept my hope alive as I continued to pray Romans 15:13. And He enabled my continuing to serve in the care and prayer ministries of our church. I began regularly to pray to be FED by God: that God would provide **F**ocus, **E**nergy, and **D**iscernment to complete tasks for that day. Each morning, during my devotional and coffee time, I would pray: "Dear God, may Your Holy Spirit give me focus and energy to do what You would have me do this day, and the discernment to know just what it is You would have me do."

God's answering that prayer was a gift He provided to carry me through that first year without succumbing to self-pity and depression. The outward focus on others instead of my own heartbreak was instrumental in enabling me to keep a promise I had made to myself regarding David.

Throughout his three-year battle with cancer, no matter how much he suffered, David absolutely did not want to be pitied. Friends would sometimes ask him if he didn't wonder, "Why me?" David's response was always, "Why not me?" He said bad things happen to many people, and many of those people have it far worse than him, so he had no right to ask "Why me?"

"Why not me?

14

David told me early on that the thing he hated the very most about his cancer was people feeling sorry for him, which he could tell by the way many people looked at and treated him. David loved interacting with people, and he wanted to be treated "normally." Thus, early on, I had to make the decision—to promise myself—not to pity my son. As a mother, it would have been easy and natural to do so, as I saw him endure hardships and suffering beyond anything I had ever experienced, not to mention my fear over things he would yet face. But I could not hide my feelings from my perceptive son; he could see them in my face, my demeanor, and my occasional tears. And so, I prayed from the outset that God help me keep my promise not to pity David. God graciously, and near miraculously, answered.

Whereas pity is the feeling of sorrow for the predicament of someone, compassion is sympathy plus the desire to help that person. Obviously, I was filled with great compassion for my son. Rather than indulge in pity, I made it a priority to do anything I could to support David and his family, to ease his suffering, and to provide encouragement and comfort. I had to learn to distinguish compassion from pity, and to realize that not pitying David did not equate to not loving him. Rather, not pitying David was the highest, and hardest, form of love I could bestow.

> Not pitying does not equate to not loving.

I remember as if it were yesterday one occasion when I thought my heart would break in anguish out of sadness for David. Since his youth, David enjoyed hunting with his dad. He had recently connected with a friend who operated a camp that was overrun by wild hogs. The friend, knowing David's love of hunting and the outdoors, offered to host David and any sidekicks for a weekend if they would come reduce the numbers of the destructive hogs. David was invigorated at the idea, and Mike was all in; it sounded far more exciting than the dove hunting they traditionally enjoyed.

Together, the two of them procured the necessary equipment and made plans. But those plans never came to fruition, because David's health took a downturn that spring. He increasingly began to struggle with low oxygen, which in turn reduced his strength and energy. Although he remained dedicated to his work, teaching his students and striving for quality time with family and friends took every ounce of his energy.

Just before Easter that spring, during an evening church service, David's decline was very much on my heart as I listened to a tenderly beautiful song. For the first time, the terrible possibility occurred to me that David might not be around the following Easter. My surroundings faded into obscurity as I silently cried to God, "God, David has such simple wants. This (the hunting weekend) is something that would give him such joy. After all his anticipation and planning, it breaks my heart to think he might never get to do it; it crushes my heart to think of all the other things he would miss out on if he should die. Please, don't let that be a possibility!"

Instantly, the thought sprang into my mind, "Nothing you miss on earth will matter in Heaven." My despair was stilled, and the thought came, very clearly, a second time, "Nothing you miss on earth will matter in Heaven."

That thought was a precious gift from God, which greatly bolstered my resolve not to pity

> "Nothing you miss on earth will matter in Heaven."

David. Remembering that truth brought me comfort through the difficult times that followed, and it continues to sustain me when I am saddened especially by news of untimely deaths.

The possibility of David's dying had never been out of my realm of reason. I had known from the outset—from experience with family members and dear friends who were strong believers and fervent prayers—that serious health battles do not always have the earthly ending we so deeply desire. Nevertheless, throughout David's battle, I never ceased to pray in great faith for God's earthly healing.

When I sometimes sensed that God might gently be preparing me for the unwelcome outcome, I prayed the only thing I knew to pray, "God, I don't know if it is You preparing my heart or the devil threatening my faith, but as long as David has breath, I will continue to pray for and claim Your earthly healing for my son."

Over the next weeks, my first serious consideration of the possibility of David's dying retreated to the back of my mind. I continued to pray in faith for David's healing. I prayed for greater faith to believe in that healing. I employed my imagination to bolster my faith, as I envisioned David years down the line progressing in his career, perhaps teaching art education at the university level, supporting his nephews in their endeavors, and walking Alexis down the wedding aisle. Those imaginings, along with my prayers and God's assurance that nothing David might miss on earth would matter in Heaven anyway, helped keep at bay both my tears and my propensity to feel sorry for him.

There were, of course, many private times when I totally broke down. But overall, I followed David's lead in seeking joy in every activity and adopting his "It's all good" attitude in the face of every challenge.

It meant the world to David. He told me two days before he passed that he didn't know how I could have been so strong, but that it had meant the world and made things much easier for him. I responded that it was through God's grace, but also because I figured if David could live without feeling sorry for himself, I owed it to him to do no less.

When David died, I told myself, "If I managed not to pity David while he was here, I refuse to do so now that he is in Heaven." I knew that was the last thing David would have wanted. Again, I asked God to help me with that resolve.

I also promised myself that, with God's continued help, I would not indulge in self-pity. If I didn't pity my son through all his suffering, I surely could not justify pitying myself.

It took daily intentionality to steer clear of pitying David or myself. It required

> It took daily intentionality to steer clear of pitying David or myself.

asking God every morning to help me—often as I toasted David with my morning cup of coffee. It required lots of talking to myself when I felt myself drifting toward feeling sorry for David or myself.

And my daily prayer for focus, energy, and discernment to serve others proved to be one of the best antidotes to combat pity. I found that focusing what little energy I had into continued service kept pity at bay when I stayed busy.

> My daily prayer for focus, energy, and discernment to serve others proved to be one of the best antidotes to combat pity.

SUMMER

Ladybugs, Tender Memories, and Gratitude

As days warmed that first spring after David's passing, and spring morphed into summer, tender memories flooded my heart and overflowed daily in tears. David had always loved the outdoors. Thus, many vivid memories of his life—from early childhood through young adulthood—were triggered by the feels and smells of early summer.

And as much joy as it brought me to picture him digging in the back yard, scooping tadpoles from an area pond, enjoying summer family camping trips, or just hanging out with friends under our back trees—every joyful memory was accompanied by that familiar sting, "Dear God, David can't really be gone!"

During his cancer battle, David had grown even more to cherish the outdoors. Year-round, but especially as warmth returned and days lengthened, David loved to grille outdoors and entertain family and friends. He worked at landscaping his yard to make it a winsome haven. He planned campouts and outdoor excursions with friends and family, especially daughter

Alexis. He took his third-grade Cub scouts on a weekend campout to a nearby state park—a joy-filled weekend that was the first outing outside Lubbock for several of his students.

He spent many days at car shows with his dad, sitting in the shade and shooting the breeze with anyone and everyone. He spent many evenings cheering for, and heckling, his dad as Mike played senior softball. He golfed whenever possible; one of his best friends later said, "It wasn't so much about golf as it was about companionship and fresh air, away from all those doctor appointments." Companionship, fresh air, and joy—that pretty much encapsulated David's love for the outdoors.

Every new season brought unique challenges of "firsts" faced without my son. The onset of that first summer ambushed me with challenges I had not anticipated, and I struggled to maintain my forward movement down the path of grief.

> Each new season brought unique challenges of "firsts" faced without my son.

God reached out to me in my struggle through the simple request from my precious 8-year-old granddaughter: "Grandma, Daddy used to take me over to my school to hunt for ladybugs. Do you think we could do that?"

My heart immediately melted. Of course, we could do that!

From the moment of David's passing, her grandpa and I had prayed continually for our precious Alexis in the loss of her dad. We had done and would continue to do anything we could to ease that loss. I jumped on this opportunity to do something our granddaughter specifically desired to do—especially something that would connect both Alexis and me with David, get us outdoors, and give us a positive focus for those long summer days.

Together, Alexis and I immediately researched how to feed and care for ladybugs. I had previously given her a butterfly habitat; now that the butterflies were grown and released, we converted it into a habitat for ladybugs. We gathered several collection containers and poked holes in the lids.

Then, we headed over to Alexis's schoolyard. She remembered just where she and her dad had found the most ladybugs, and sure enough, we found several on our first ladybug hunting expedition. She showed me how her daddy had taught her patiently to get the ladybugs to crawl on her hand, and then ever so gently to ease them into the collection container—being especially careful when attaching the lid so as not to squish any ladybugs that crawled to the top.

The weather that first day was gorgeous. It was warm, but not hot—just perfect in the shade of the sheltering trees. The freshly distinctive smell of early summer wafted on a gentle breeze. The feel of tender leaves of grass between our fingers and the tickle of ladybugs as they crawled on our hands delighted our senses. Both time and grief slipped into a more relaxed mode as God refreshed our hearts with the simple joys of His creation.

And so ensued what I have come to remember as "the summer of the ladybugs."

Alexis's schoolyard was but the first of our ladybug hunting locales. Throughout that summer, we scoured promising areas all around town in search of ladybug treasure troves. Her dad had also taken her ladybug hunting at one of the elementary schools where he had taught. She again remembered just where to look—this time in dense patches of clover; and indeed, our efforts yielded several ladybugs to add to her habitat, replacing the ladybugs we regularly released into our backyards.

I was blessed to spend much time with Alexis over that summer, as her grandpa and I cared for her part of most weekdays and transported her to activities her mom had arranged. She attended some morning camps on the Texas Tech University campus. Each day when I picked her up, we checked out different locations around the sprawling, grassy campus—now looking especially for prolific areas of green clover. We drove to areas near the American Windmill Museum, where Mike volunteered, and found some great ladybug hideouts.

And so ensued what I have come to remember as "the summer of the ladybugs."

Basically, wherever we went that summer, we always were on the lookout for places we could check out for ladybugs. Our joint mission provided a positive focus that helped lighten the weight of grief.

Alexis's delight with ladybug hunts was contagious. I felt stirrings of joy that I had not felt since David passed, and I often imagined David smiling and cheering us on as he watched our efforts. Top all that off with the healing power of the outdoors, which had been so important to David, and I sensed God leading us tenderly on through that first year of grief.

God also carried me through that tender first summer by reminding me of blessings. A quote I read early on in a grief devotional book had stuck with me. It went something like, "We have so many things for which to be thankful; there's just that one hard thing." Recognizing the truth of that statement in our circumstances, I resolved daily to be more aware of, and thank God for, all our blessings—whether mundane or extraordinary.

God, as He so often did in response to my cries and questions, gave me a thought that comforted me early on and continues to sustain me: "Do not focus on what you lack or have lost. Rather, be thankful for what you have and are promised as God's child."

I repeated that principle again and again to myself through those early seasons of grief, and I often still need the wise reminder. Some sight or smell or circumstance will suddenly remind me of David, or cause me to wonder what he would be doing and what

> "Do not focus on what you lack or have lost. Rather, be thankful for what you have and are promised as God's child."

all he would have accomplished if he were still here. As my heart fills with that familiar ache of loss, I am tempted to go down the path of focusing on his absence—on what we lack and have lost. Instead, by God's grace, I am prompted instead to thank God for the years we had with our amazing son, for the joy he brought to people from all walks of life, and for the lasting impact he made in the lives of his family, his students, his friends, and even strangers; although, as one of his closest friends reminds us, "David never met a stranger."

During those earliest seasons of grief, I was also inspired by my husband Mike, who by God's grace intuitively adopted two practices that fostered my awareness of blessings. The first was his straightforward thankfulness; every time we prayed together—whether at mealtime or otherwise—he began (and still begins) with, "God we are so blessed." Considering how devastated he was by the loss of David, who was not just his only son, but also had become his closest friend—it was deeply touching and highly inspiring that he remained so genuinely thankful for the many blessings God has given us.

The second of Mike's practices was his response to the inevitably frequent question from family, friends, and acquaintances: "How are you doing?" That question, which is asked out of caring concern, is so very difficult to answer. But Mike intuitively came up with the perfect and fitting response which has become his trademark, by which he is known among all our church family and friends: "It is well with my soul." I love my husband for many reasons, but that consistent response, which is deeply genuine in spite of his hurting heart, always comforts me and warms my heart.

> "It is well with my soul."

With a mindset of thankfulness, I doubled down that first summer on my resolve to be intentionally grateful. I had begun a gratitude journal soon after David's passing at the advice of a dear friend who lost a daughter three years prior. I found great comfort in thinking of and writing down things about my son for which I was grateful—even things related to his cancer battle, hospitalization, and passing.

I spent time that summer re-reading and adding to the gratitude journal I had started. Looking back, the first few entries, which I had written soon after David's passing, were short, succinct, and very telling. They are just a few of many examples of how God gradually led me more and more to recognize His love and mercy in what seemed the worst of times.

Gratitude Journal for David:
First Entries

- **New Life for David.** "New life, healing, no cancer"—my overarching prayer for David the past many weeks. I praise God for answering—though not as I was thinking. Please God, help me to live this life well without him.
- **David's Last Weeks on Earth.** For treasured memories in the hospital with David his last two weeks. He prayed for strength, courage, and grace to "do this." God answered that prayer and graciously allowed me to witness the character of the man my son had become. I am eternally grateful for that.
- **David's Contagious Smile.** His love of life shows so in his last pictures. I can vividly picture his smile and wink, even behind oxygen apparatus, when I would look at him with concern these past weeks. I can only imagine his smile now!!

As I continued journaling, things for which I was grateful expanded beyond recent memories to cover a lifetime, including the amazing legacy he left his students and his daughter. Re-reading what I had already written refreshed my joy as I smiled through tears over memories from childhood to adulthood to David's final days.

I prayed for God to help me recall fresh memories to record in my ongoing journal, and He was gracious to do so. Motivated by ladybug outings to seek solace in nature, I took many long walks that summer. It was often on those walks, while talking with God, that I would recall more memories that spurred me to gratitude.

It took me a while to find comfort in memories and pictures of David's childhood. As much as I wanted to remember, it simply hurt too much early on in the grief process. But as gradually the joy of remembering his life came to outweigh the pain of missing him, I was able to recall more and more.

> But as gradually the joy of remembering his life came to outweigh the pain of missing him, I was able to recall more and more.

One of the memories I recalled on one of my walks was humorously coincidental to that ladybug summer. When he was about three, David came running in from the back yard with his sister Carolyn. They were agitated and scared, and it took a few minutes for Mike, me, and my parents (who were visiting) to figure out what David meant by excitedly repeating, "It hurts my ear. I can feel it moving. I don't know what it is. It tickles; it hurts." We surmised, to my horror, that something alive was in his ear.

Following the "bug in ear" instructions from our handy first aid book, we soothed David and positioned his head in his grandmother's lap; and after a couple drops of baby oil, out scampered a ladybug. I was super relieved, as I had feared a much more menacing insect. We let David and Carolyn observe the rescued critter before we all took it out in the back yard to set it free.

I was grateful for that fun memory, and I was doubly grateful for the serendipitous connection with our ladybug summer. It was as if, in a way, God was bringing full circle the cycles of our lives. And I took it as a reminder that life indeed goes on, as David would have been the first to point out.

I will always remember that first summer without David as "the summer of the ladybugs." As I look back through my even-more-enhanced lens of gratitude, I view it as a treasured season that brought healing and additional stirrings of the joy God was working to restore in our lives. It was one of the most visible ways God answered my Romans 15:13 prayer that He would not let us lose our hope.

In my still all-too-encompassing grief, I found myself more and more praising God for the wonders of His creation. I thanked Him especially for the comforting sensations of the beautiful outdoors, and specifically for fresh air, companionship, and ladybugs.

Early Fall

Setbacks, Prayer,
and Fellow Climbers

My ladybug summer provided a much-needed balm for my soul, for which I will forever be grateful. I had no unrealistic expectations that it would short-cut my grieving, however. That truth became painfully obvious with the first signs of fall.

Having grown up in a family of educators—my mom being a home economics teacher and dad being a teacher-then-superintendent—fall had always seemed more like the start of a new year than January 1. Fall brought a sense of excitement and new beginnings, lots of preparations and purchases, and start-of-school schedules and activities. That sense carried through adulthood as most of my work career was spent in education, and it grew even more when David started teaching art in elementary school.

One of my most fun adult connections with David was our love for students and teaching. After my parents died, no one else in the family shared those education interests. As he neared college graduation and began classroom internship experiences, David would come over and talk for hours about his students and lessons and experiences; it was obvious he had found his ideal career calling. After he started teaching, that connection between us strengthened.

In my previous work life, I had worked on statewide committees to develop the most recent curriculum standards for Texas schools, so I was familiar with the Texas Essential Knowledge and Skills (TEKS) for each grade level. I had worked on curriculum adaptations for students with special needs, so I was well familiar with the Individualized Education Program (IEP) that could be developed as needed by the Admission, Review, and Dismissal (ARD) committee. David had many students with special needs, and he was deeply committed to reaching and teaching every one of his students, from kindergarten through fifth grade. We would spend hours in my living room talking about TEKS and IEPs and ARDs, plus other education acronyms. His dad, knowing none of the secret lingo, would retreat to another room.

My love for education, coupled with my delight in witnessing David's love for his students, motivated me to support his teaching efforts in every way possible. I volunteered at his school, helping in his classroom when he had special projects that required extra hands. I assisted with the Cub scout troop he led after school one day a week, and Mike and I both went along as additional sponsors on a weekend campout David planned for the troop at an area state park. When he had to miss school, I typed up substitute lesson plans while he dictated.

I share these connections so you might understand why that first fall was so hard. As the start of school approached, I daily was reminded that I would otherwise have been helping David set up his classroom. The first day of school, I was painfully aware that I would have eagerly been awaiting his certain visit to tell me all about the day.

As fall days progressed, I knew I would have been helping with his students, typing up lesson plans, or helping David and his dad put together some grand art project. But instead, my heart breaking, I grieved his absence. I grieved the special education connections that only David shared with me. I grieved all the future joys of connection that now would never occur.

That fall was exceptionally hard, and it wasn't just the education connections. Fall was filled with special family memories over our children's lifetimes, and everywhere I turned, each new activity was yet

> Everywhere I turned, each new activity was yet another reminder that David was no longer here.

another reminder that David was no longer here. Fall was extra hard on Mike as well, because it was tied to the September start-up of dove hunting season, and bowling leagues, and a myriad of other activities Mike and David had shared. Thus, my heart not only hurt for myself, but also for Mike, who so deeply missed his son.

A few years later, I penned a short poem to express the heightened grief that still besets me as fall approaches and I watch the leaves beginning to turn yellow-orange through my kitchen window each morning.

> ## ~ ~ FALL ~ ~
> Each year as summer's winding down,
>   and back-to-school is in the air,
> I sometimes still will turn around,
>   expecting I will see you there.
> My heart aches softly in the fall,
>   for then I miss you most of all.

Just as the sensations of summer had provided comfort and healing, so the sensations of fall brought a fierce resurgence of grief. More frequently than I had in months, I found myself thinking, mouthing, whispering, or crying out, "Dear God. David can't really be gone!"

It is easy to understand, looking back, that this "setback" should not have been surprising. In fact, it really was not a setback, because getting through grief is by no means a straight upward progression. The plot line of grief is shaped like a roller-coaster. The overall momentum is hopefully upward, but it typically progresses via wavy inclines and sharp—sometimes stomach-churning—falls.

Recognizing this as one of many resurgences of grief, I basically went back to square one.

> The plot line of grief is shaped like a roller-coaster... it typically progresses via wavy inclines and sharp, sometimes stomach-churning, falls.

Recalling those early days of loss, I reverted when needed to reminding myself of each next step—one step at a time. I was intentional to seek comfort in my morning coffee and devotional time, writing entries in my gratitude journal, and keeping up my volunteer activities at church.

Monthly prayer articles for our church newsletter, which I had begun writing shortly before David became ill, continued to keep me focused on prayer practices that drew me closer to God, and I clung in faith to the promise in James 4:8, *"Draw near to God, and He will draw near to you."*

It was in this season that God began to stir in my heart the desire to write a book that would encourage others to try some of the simple prayer practices that I found so helpful along my path of grief. It would be four more years before that book, *Prayer Matters*, came to fruition. But the things God taught me about prayer in my grief not only carried me through those early seasons, but have continued to enrich my life and faith, and I expect with certainty will carry me through to the end of my journey.

I was thankful that fall for having acquired some skills to cope with the stomach-churning falls in the roller coaster of grief, because I relied heavily on every helpful one. As I took long walks, my mind flashed back to my long walks near David's hospital; as I had then, I prayed Romans 15:13 over and over. "Dear God, I so terribly miss David. I know I must grieve, but please, don't let me lose hope."

From the very beginning, God provided one of the best resources through which He answered my prayer. He had pre-provided a network of friends and family whose care and compassion would support Mike and me and our family through every step of our grief journey. Looking back through my calendar for that first fall, I notice that days were beginning to fill back in with lunches with a friend or gatherings or weekend trips. We had continued to socialize, especially with church friends and family, even in our earliest days of grief; but often, our hearts had not been fully able to engage. Now, we were beginning to enjoy that companionship more, as gradually we became more able temporarily to slip off the mantle of grief.

> Gradually we became more able temporarily to slip off the mantle of grief.

We were, and continue to be, blessed with a large and caring Christian family. We love and are grateful for each one of them; and every one of them has helped ease our journey of grief.

But it is at times like that first fall season, when grief is unexpectedly tender, that I especially crave—and God always graciously provides—connections with "fellow climbers." That is a term I somewhere read to describe people who also are climbing a similar hard road of life and grief, and who are willing and wanting to help others along the same hard road. Fellow climbers well understand the pitfalls along the way. Those who have progressed higher up the climb can call back encouragement to those behind, or at times extend a hand to help the lagging climber over the next rocky crag.

Grief can feel agonizingly lonely, and it is easy even to surmise at times that few others have hurt so badly. The truth, of course, is that grief is one of the most common of human experiences, and many people, even within our fairly immediate circles, are

> Grief can feel agonizingly lonely, and it is easy even to surmise at times that few others have hurt so badly.

enduring losses we know nothing about. Making connections with some of those fellow climbers can be an exceptional gift. Such connections have potential to dispel that sensation of aloneness in grief. They also open our hearts to receive comfort from and extend comfort to others along the path. And they protect against the self-pity trap of falsely thinking we have it so much worse than most.

In every season of grief I have experienced, I have been comforted by fellow climbers. When my Mom died from cancer 25 years ago, God connected me with people who had recently grieved the loss of a parent—and several, specifically, their mothers. When my Daddy died fourteen years later, I was again comforted by others who had lost a parent—including many who had followed almost our same long road through Alzheimer's.

> In every season of grief I have experienced, I have been comforted by fellow climbers.

Fellow climbers to whom I was drawn like a magnet that first fall after David's passing were a subgroup who share a bond none of us ever imagined we would face—the loss of a child. Two of my dearest friends happened to share that sad bond. Being a few years ahead of me on the path, they had offered love and comfort throughout David's cancer battle and since his passing. I instinctively reached to them for extra strength through that especially difficult stretch.

They offered words of comfort. They shared wisdom gleaned through their grief. Mostly, they just listened. But there was more; just being around them was a significant source of the hope for which I prayed.

I knew without a doubt that their hearts ached intensely for the children they had lost. When asked, "How do you mend a broken heart?" one replied, "You don't. You just learn to live with it." They were farther down the path of learning to live with it. And I thought, "That will be me in a few years. I will always miss David, but life—which is blessed even now—will one day feel full again."

In addition to those two friends, God placed in my path, and in Mike's, other fellow climbers who had experienced similar losses. God also was already placing us in the paths of parents whose grief was even more fresh than ours, giving us opportunity to practice 2 Corinthians 1:3–4 by comforting others with the same comfort we had experienced.

One thing fellow climbers are especially kind to do is remember the special days that are so tender to grieving hearts. Some of my

> One thing fellow climbers are especially kind to do is remember the special days that are so tender to grieving hearts.

fellow climbers are faithful each year to send a text or card on the anniversary of David's passing, which I remember as his "eternal birthday." Some also acknowledge his earthly birthday. It is a huge comfort to know they are thinking of me, it warms my heart to know they remember David, and it strengthens me to know they understand how tender such remembrance days can be. Learning from their example, I note special remembrance days of others on my calendar and in my daily devotional book, so I may be prompted to pass along gifts of remembrance to others.

> Learning from their example, I note special remembrance days of others on my calendar and in my daily devotional book, so I may be prompted to pass along gifts of remembrance to others.

As days counted down to the first anniversary of David's passing, I thanked God frequently for the fellow climbers in my life. As I did so on one occasion, God brought to mind a memory that took my early grief journey back to the very beginning.

My mind flashed back to David's 29th birthday, which was the day his biopsy revealed cancer. After surgery, he had been put in a hospital room to recover for several hours before being dismissed. Numb with shock, when the opportunity arose, I slipped away down the hall to an empty room on the near-empty floor where I could pray, process, and cry.

I vividly remember crying out in desperation: "God, if David should die, I don't see how we could go on."

And just as vividly, I remember the instant response that sprang into my mind, "Both of your grandmothers lost children."

That thought stunned me. Yes, come to think of it, both of my grandmothers had lost a child at a fairly early age. Daddy's mother lost a son who had been born with a heart defect and struggled to live to late childhood. Mother's mom lost a young adult daughter who was very close to David's age when she passed. I had known of both instances, but I never really gave them much thought. It was before I was in the picture, and I had only known and remembered my grandmothers as full of life and love and joy—always welcoming and hosting and busily caring for our big family crew.

For the first time, I thought about the grief each of them surely had suffered, and I felt a twinge of regret that I had never acknowledged their losses.

I heard God's message loud and clear, and it resonated in my spirit. A flood of memories flashed through my mind of wonderful times with my grandmothers, and I knew in my heart that if, by the grace of God, they could survive losing their children and go on to live such full lives, then by that same grace, I surely could as well.

I did not sense that God was telling me early on that David would die, but rather I sensed Him quelling my instinctive fear and bringing to mind the perfect role models for the battle that loomed ahead—my beloved grandmothers. I continued to think about both of my grandmothers often through the ups and downs of David's subsequent battle. I even had a few conversations with them in my mind.

The night David passed, I clung to the reassurance they both had survived such a night. Now, as David's eternal birthday neared, I told myself they both had likewise passed that milestone. I regularly pictured in my mind's eye, when they would have been some years down their roads of grief, the vibrant and joyful women I knew as my grandmothers. And I resolved anew, "If they got through it, I can too."

> "If they got through it, I can too."

THE FIRST ANNIVERSARY

And Beyond

The first anniversary was a milestone on my journey of grief. As I recalled those earliest days, I could see how far I had come. Although tears still were just beneath the surface, I had become able on most occasions to postpone weeping until I was alone.

The mantle of grief was always present, but the weight had begun to lighten ever so slightly. Although there was never a time when I did not feel an ache in my heart, that sharp pain in my gut was less frequent and much less intense. Looking back, I could see definite progress. Encouraged that Mike and I had made it that far, I had faith that God would faithfully lead us through.

However, looking ahead, it was still incredibly hard to imagine the long road of years ahead without David. It would be several more years before I would cease being ambushed by the realization that he was gone from our earthly lives and would not be present for any of the future experiences I had always assumed we would share.

There is a little book entitled *Love You Forever*. It begins with a mother rocking her infant son, singing that she would love him forever: "As long as

Looking ahead, it was still incredibly hard to imagine the long road of years ahead without David.

I'm living, my baby you'll be." It progresses through the son's becoming a man, until near the end, he picks up his frail, aged mom and sings, as he rocks her back and forth, that he will forever love her: "As long as I'm living, my Mommy you'll be."

David gave the book to me one Mother's Day during the seven years that Mike and I cared for my dad as he progressed through stages of Alzheimer's. Since we all lived in Lubbock, David was very attentive to his Pop during those years. He often visited him, and he always met me at the hospital any time Daddy was sent via ambulance due to a fall or other medical issue. I would jokingly tell David to get in practice, because I expected the same attention one day—hence, the gifted book.

As I wrap up the writing of this book, we have recently passed the ten-year anniversary of David's passing to eternal life. To this day, I cannot read any part of *Love You Forever* without blubbering, and I doubt I ever can. It seems inconceivable that I will so long outlive my son, and of all the experiences I dread facing without David, those final years of my own life are perhaps the worst. It is a selfish and unreasonable fear, especially given that I am blessed with a very loving and capable daughter and three grandchildren, who—assuming the natural cycles of life play out—will be there to care for me as David and I were for my dad. But it is nevertheless one of the fears that most tempts me to feel sorry for myself.

And so, I revert to reminding myself after what is now ten years, as I did in those earliest months of grief, of my promise to pity neither David nor myself. And I continue to pursue practices that have helped me from the outset to move forward.

> I continue to pursue practices that have helped me from the outset to move forward.

I still look forward each day to my morning routine of coffee and time in God's word. I treasure in my heart God's many promises in Scriptures, such as those I have quoted in this book.

I still set aside time every Sunday evening to look through calendared commitments for the upcoming week, transferring them to my listing under "Family" and "Serving God." As I fill in my daily to-do chart, I remember to thank God for the meaningful tasks that provide such fulfillment, and which I pray bring extra blessings to others. Daily, I continue to pray that God will grant me focus, energy, and discernment to do the things He calls me to do.

I frequently remind myself of wise thoughts God gave me and Mike through David's battle and those early years of grief, often in response to my questioning or crying out to Him. "There are no hospitals in Heaven." "Nothing we miss on earth will matter in Heaven." "It is well with my soul." "If they got through it, I can too." "Do not focus on what you lack or have lost. Rather, be thankful for what you have and are promised as God's child."

I find strength in focusing in gratitude on what I have.

I am daily refreshed by the wonders of God's creation as I watch seasons change through the view from my kitchen table as I meet God there each morning.

I find joy in looking forward to the promise through belief in Jesus Christ of life eternal in God's perfect new creation — where there will be no more death or mourning or crying or pain (Revelation 21:4).

> I find joy in looking forward to the promise through belief in Jesus Christ of life eternal in God's perfect new creation— where there will be no more death or mourning or crying or pain (Revelation 21:4).

I find delight in imagining what life in God's eternal kingdom will be like, in wondering what all will be included in the things that *"no eye has seen, no ear has heard, and no human mind has conceived—the things God has prepared for those who love Him"* (1 Corinthians 2:9).

I cannot know for sure what wondrous things we will get to see and do and enjoy in Heaven. Among the first, I expect a welcoming hug from my son, and I envision his big David smile as he greets me. I can imagine him saying, with a huge grin, "It's wonderfully ironic that, after all you have told me about Jesus and Heaven, I am the one who gets to show you around."

I expect among the many marvels I'll get to see will be stunningly colorful skies, amazingly beautiful vegetation, and myriads of wonderful creatures. Among them, I sure hope there will be—I really think there will be—ladybugs.

And I heard a loud voice from the throne saying, "Look! God's dwelling place is now among the people, and He will dwell with them. They will be His people, and God himself will be with them and be their God. He will wipe every tear from their eyes. There will be no more death' or mourning or crying or pain, for the old order of things has passed away."
~ Revelation 21:3–4

However, as it is written: "What no eye has seen, what no ear has heard, and what no human mind has conceived"—the things God has prepared for those who love Him...
~ 1 Corinthians 2:9

BONUS SECTION

For Further Reflection or Discussion

I journaled the first draft of this short book three years ago, primarily as an outlet for a resurgence of missing David that hit me during the Covid lockdown. Writing is my therapy, my means of reflection, my way of working through things, and my way of organizing thoughts I think might help others.

I have prayed for months to discern whether it is something that should be published or filed away and discarded upon my own passing, along with other journal entries that God has inspired for my personal growth and healing.

I eventually decided, after input from a few trusted fellow climbers, to publish. This section is provided as a bonus for those who might wish further to reflect on principles and practices that have helped me, either alone or with a group. Many questions are worded for you to explore and share additional principles and practices you, or members of your group, have discovered.

It is my prayer that God will use *Summer of the Ladybugs* to comfort others in this common journey of grief.

*"Praise be to the God and Father of our
Lord Jesus Christ, the Father of
compassion and the God of all comfort, who
comforts us in all our troubles, so that we
can comfort those in any trouble with the
comfort we ourselves receive from God."*
~ 2 Corinthians 1:3–4

LATE FALL: Pain, Disbelief, and God's Mercy

1. Describe your experience with pain and disbelief in the early days after the death of someone you love dearly.

2. How did you attempt to cope with that initial, gut-wrenching sense of loss?

3. Even in the darkest of times before and after the passing of your dear one, what evidences of God's mercy can you see? (If you have a hard time seeing many, or any, that is OK. Keep this question open, and keep your heart open to God. Ask God to show you in hindsight, over time, how His hand has been with you throughout.)

4. Reflect on Romans 15:13: *May the God of hope fill you with all joy and peace as you trust in Him, so that you may overflow with hope by the power of the Holy Spirit.* What helped you find hope in the early days of grief?

WINTER: One Foot in Front of the Other, Routine, and Mornings in God's Word

5. Describe your experience with being unable fully to function in the aftermath of great loss. Can you identify with the need to take one step at a time, one foot in front of the other? Give examples of how that might look in your day.

6. What tasks seem easiest to continue while in the early throes of grief? What tasks seem most difficult? What helps with both?

7. Have you found that routine can be a welcome friend in stressful times? Share routines that you find helpful and even comforting. What are some additional routines you might cultivate to help you get through various parts of your day?

8. Describe how you approach mornings. What helps you set a positive tone for each day?

9. Share helpful suggestions for getting through the first few months of grief.

SPRING: One Week at a Time, Serving Others, and Rejecting Self-Pity

10. How does grief impact your ability to plan and keep up with commitments? What has helped you in planning and fulfilling tasks and commitments each week?

11. What tasks continue to be doable and meaningful when you are grieving? What tasks seem difficult or impossible?

12. Begin to note things you do for others, such as volunteer work, helping in church programs, or writing notes or calling folks who need contact. Do these help lighten your grief, at least while you are occupied with serving? What are some ways you might expand the time you spend serving others?

13. Reflect on things you used to do that are especially hard to do after loss of a loved one—perhaps especially hard when doing them for the first time. How do you cope with these times? What might help you or someone else through these "firsts"?

14. Reflect on the principle of 2 Corinthians 1:3–4, that the comfort you received in grief now enables you to comfort others. How does this verse apply to your experience? (If you haven't yet experienced any application, keep this question open as you watch for opportunities to help others benefit from what you have learned in times of suffering and grief.)

15. It is common in grief to experience lack of focus and energy, as well as difficulty making decisions and discerning what to do. Try praying specifically for God to grant focus, energy, and discernment—to be FED by God. As you do this over time, reflect on your experience.

16. It is a common human reaction to feel pity for a loved one who is suffering, and for ourself as we grieve a loved one's passing. How can this be detrimental?

17. Reflect on the quote: "Not pitying someone does not equate to not loving that dear one." Explain the difference between pity and compassion, and give an example of how each might look in action.

18. Describe your experience with both pity and self-pity. What are some ways you might redirect your feelings of pity into positive acts of compassion? What are some ways you can combat the urge to indulge in self-pity?

19. "Nothing we miss on earth will matter in Heaven." How does that thought help you with questions and regrets over loved ones who have passed?

SUMMER: Ladybugs, Tender Memories, and Gratitude

20. What seasons have been especially hard as you grieve your dear one? Why?

21. What helps you deal with these especially hard seasons?

22. What good memories do you recall in association with the outdoors? What outdoor settings or activities bring you comfort as you walk through grief?

23. List some possibilities for adding outdoor settings or activities to your life that might provide additional comfort.

24. "Do not focus on what you lack or have lost. Rather, be thankful for what you have and are promised as God's child." Think about this statement, and ask God to help you practice it through the coming week. Then, reflect on whether and how it was helpful.

25. List blessings for which you remain thankful, even as you grieve. Add other things to this list as they come to mind. Take time frequently to meditate on, and thank God for, each blessing.

26. Challenge yourself to find things related to your dear one's passing for which you can, in retrospect, be thankful. It may be hard at first, but the more open you are to seeing how God's love and mercy were active even in what seemed the worst of times, the more you can find things for which to be thankful. As you do, express—preferably in writing—your thanks to God.

27. Be intentional often to praise God for the wonders of His creation. Take time to view a sunset or a sunrise. Find places that expose you to whatever you find beautiful and comforting in nature. Take times to sit and rest, weep if it helps, and soak in at least a bit of healing.

EARLY FALL: Setbacks, Prayer, and Fellow Climbers

28. Describe setbacks or relapses you have experienced on your grief journey. What triggered them? How did you cope?

29. Does it help you to picture the plot life of grief as a roller coaster, rather than an upward-moving line? Elaborate.

30. What has been your experience with prayer as you walk the path of grief?

31. What fellow climbers have provided encouragement and eased the loneliness of your grief? Who have you had opportunity likewise to encourage?

32. What special days are most tender to your grieving heart? What helps you get through those days?

33. How might you extend comfort by remembering others on their special days? Jot down some ideas, note dates, and plan to put those ideas into action.

34. Reflect on family or friends, like the author's grandmothers, whose prior suffering and grief you may never even have considered, but who moved on to live full lives. What might you learn from them?

THE FIRST ANNIVERSARY AND BEYOND

35. Wherever you currently may be in your journey of grief, recall and reflect on how far you have come since the earliest days. What are some steps you have taken? What are some ways your grief has lightened? The idea is to focus on progress you can see as you look back to where you started.

36. What are the biggest hurdles you still face as you grieve, or as you look ahead to life without your dear one? What old or new tools might you employ to help you face these hurdles?

37. At this point in your journey, what are things that bring you joy, to which you look forward each day? From what routines, practices, or thoughts do you draw daily strength? As you share with others, aim to pick up a few new ideas to add to your toolbox.

38. Reflect on Scriptures that point to life eternal in God's perfect new creation. What do you find most comforting? What are you looking forward to in Heaven? (Even though we cannot know for sure, I think it is beneficial to imagine Heaven. And I believe no matter what wondrous things we imagine, the reality will be far more wonderful!)

Epilogue

If you are grieving, take heart. Especially if you are fairly early in this journey, be intentional to keep moving, one step at a time. If you fall back for a while, needing rest, that's OK. But get back on the road soon; putting one foot in front of the other, begin again to move forward.

Seek small, everyday comforts—a cup of coffee, a conversation with a friend, or a simple task that provides welcome distraction. Find other fellow climbers; draw strength from those ahead of you, and call back to encourage those behind.

Be open to, and expect, God to send times of refreshing; when they come, breathe them in. Trust that grief will lighten.

And do not be concerned that your loved one might fade from memory; that will never happen. Even though grief will lighten, rest assured that your love for the one who has passed will not. Rather, be encouraged that as sweet recollections gradually come to overshadow heartache, your memories will forge a deeper, sweeter connection with the one you so deeply love and miss.

Do not be concerned that your loved one might fade from memory; that will never happen. Even though grief will lighten, rest assured that your love for the one who has passed will not. Rather, be encouraged that as sweet recollections gradually come to overshadow heartache, your memories will forge a deeper, sweeter connection with the one you so deeply love and miss.

About the Author

It has always been Marilyn's desire to share with others helpful things she learns. Because writing extends that desire to a broader audience, she likewise loves to write. She was blessed in the last 20 years of her "paid career" to work with educators to develop Family and Consumer Sciences public school curriculum.

But it was after retirement, while volunteering in church prayer and care ministries, that she discerned what helpful things personally to share in books—life lessons imparted as God led her through hard seasons.

Her first book, *Prayer Matters*, stems from church newsletter articles that were written during her son's cancer battle and subsequent passing. It presents simple and practical practices that many attest to enriching their prayer lives. An accompanying *Study Guide and Journal* affords opportunity to delve more deeply.

This new book, *Summer of the Ladybugs*, encourages fellow climbers who are grieving, with special emphasis on getting through those difficult early seasons, which are filled with so many tender "firsts."

Marilyn Wragg currently lives in Lubbock, Texas, with her husband, Mike, where they are actively involved in First Christian Church. They are blessed in their immediate earthly family with a married daughter and son-in-law, a daughter-in-law, and three beloved grandchildren, as well as their son, who now resides in Heaven.